This book belongs to

.... *

* By signing here, you have agreed to be part of a scientific
experiment in which all the molecules in your body will be
temporarily rearranged.

There are nearly eight billion of us humans.

That's 8,000,000,000 bodies breathing, eating, scratching their armpits and consuming resources, and 8,000,000,000 brains thinking, feeling, falling in love and pondering the universe. All at the same time.

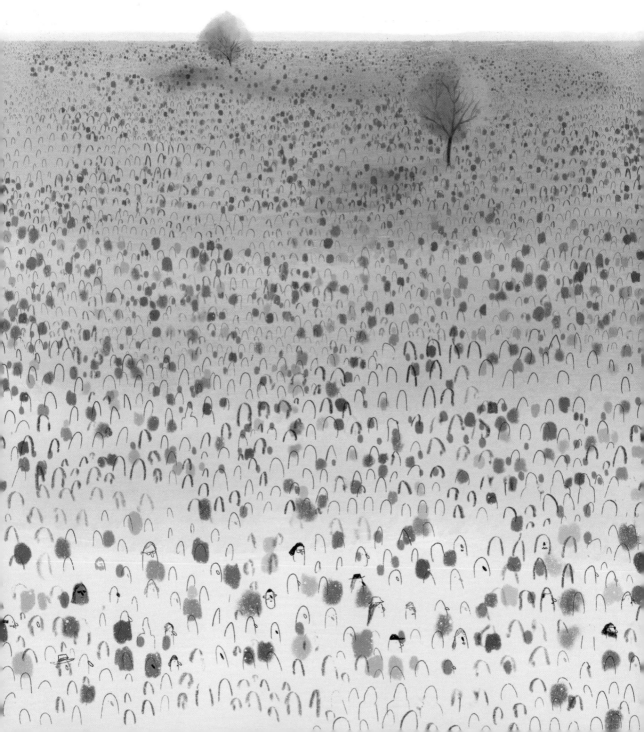

Try saying, 'Hello, nice to meet you!' ten times in a row.
Then another ten. And then another ten.

Boring, isn't it?

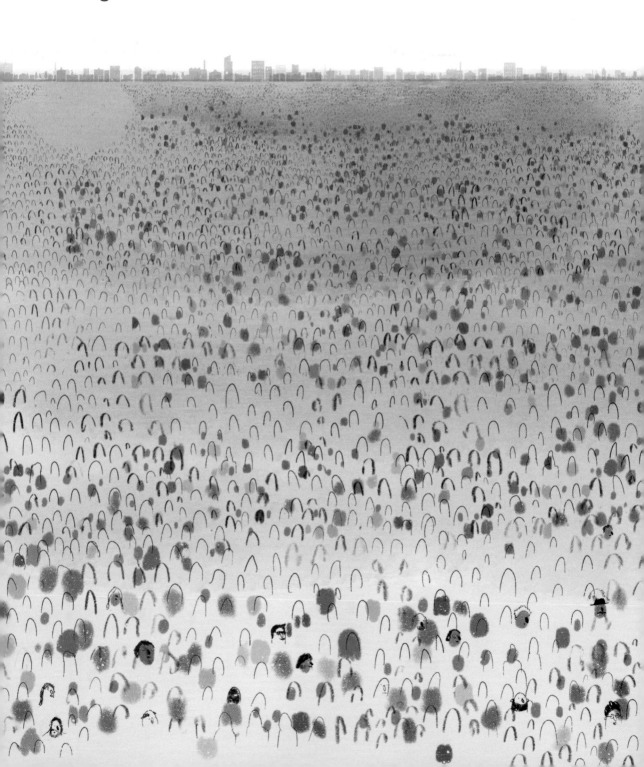

Well, to meet everybody on the planet, you'd need to keep doing that, day and night, for the next thousand years.

What a gigantic tribe we are.

On the other hand, it's been calculated that if all humanity gathered in one place, we could crowd into an area the size of Greater London. Which makes us seem like a fairly insignificant bunch after all.

It's standing room only, but all humanity fits inside this little pink circle. Put your thumb over it and you could squish the entire human race – hey, stop that!

So wait a minute . . . is eight billion people a lot or isn't it?

The trouble is, our brains haven't changed much since we lived in small groups in caves and counted on our hands and feet. We just aren't cut out to make sense of giant numbers – which makes it hard for us to understand the true scale of our species.

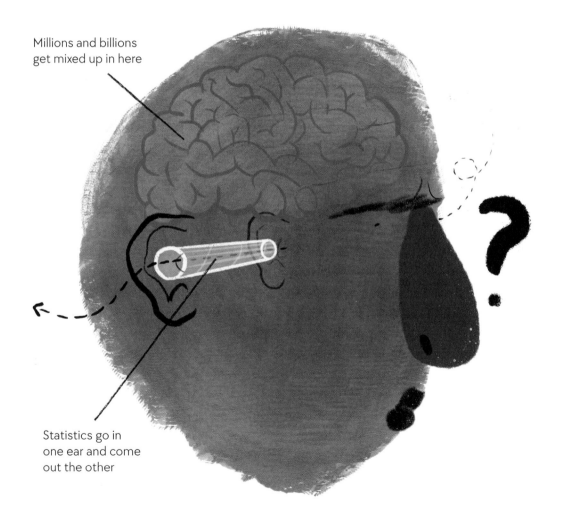

Millions and billions get mixed up in here

Statistics go in one ear and come out the other

But let's not give up on grasping how big we are just yet. We've got another idea to try.

Imagine eight plasticine people, all three centimetres tall and one centimetre wide.

You could smoosh them together into a lump and sculpt the lump into a magnificent plasticine giant, a whopping six centimetres tall and two centimetres wide.

Now, what if we did a version of this experiment with eight billion people? Instead of picturing a brain-meltingly high number of individuals, we'd only have to picture one giant.

Of course, no one would ever try an experiment like this with real people, let alone the entire population of the planet . . .

. . . *or would they??*

Behold the Smooshing Machine™!

A marvel of science and engineering, built to bring
humankind together – literally.

Entire population of the world
enters here (so that's what
everyone was queuing for) . . .

Professor Janet McCrackers of the University of Barking, inventor of the Smooshing Machine

. . . and exits in an exciting new form here.

Here we come! From the Smooshing Machine's ginormous nozzle, the most colossal foot is emerging . . .

. . . followed by a body as big as a mountain range . . .

. . . and finally, out pops the hugest of heads.

It worked! Humanity has been reborn as the 'mega human', a single being made from everyone on the planet. And we're about to stand up for the first time and reveal our full, majestic size.

Ta-da!

What a glorious specimen we are!

Feeling a bit weird after our transformation, sure, but just LOOK at us!

Height: About 3km*

Weight: 390 million tonnes (and rising by about 100kg per second)

Sex: Indeterminate (49.6% genetically female, 50.4% genetically male)

Pronouns: We/us

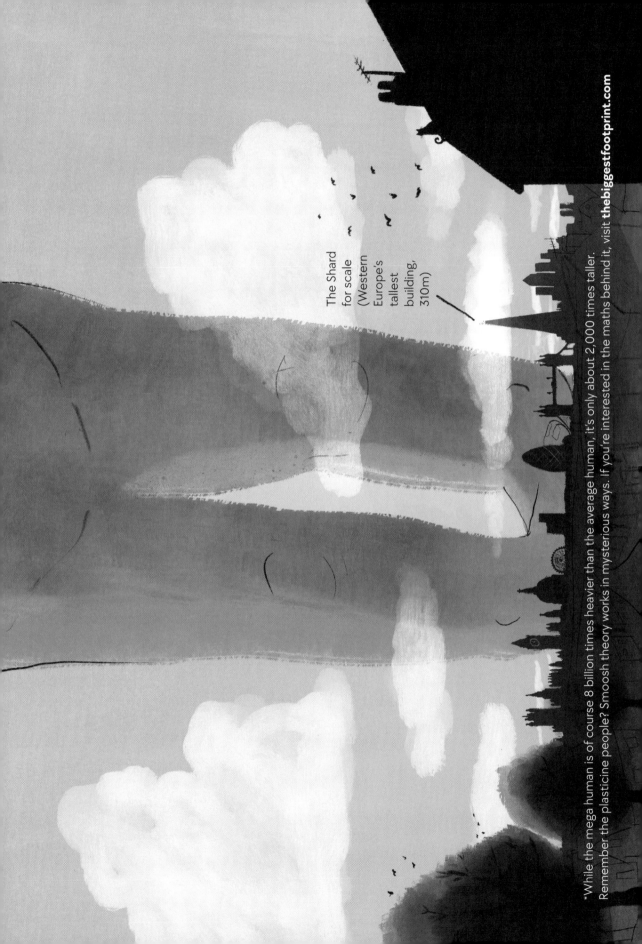

The Shard
for scale
(Western
Europe's
tallest
building,
310m)

*While the mega human is of course 8 billion times heavier than the average human, it's only about 2,000 times taller.
Remember the plasticine people? Smoosh theory works in mysterious ways. If you're interested in the maths behind it, visit **thebiggestfootprint.com**

Goodness gracious us. Our new mega eyes are as big as football pitches.

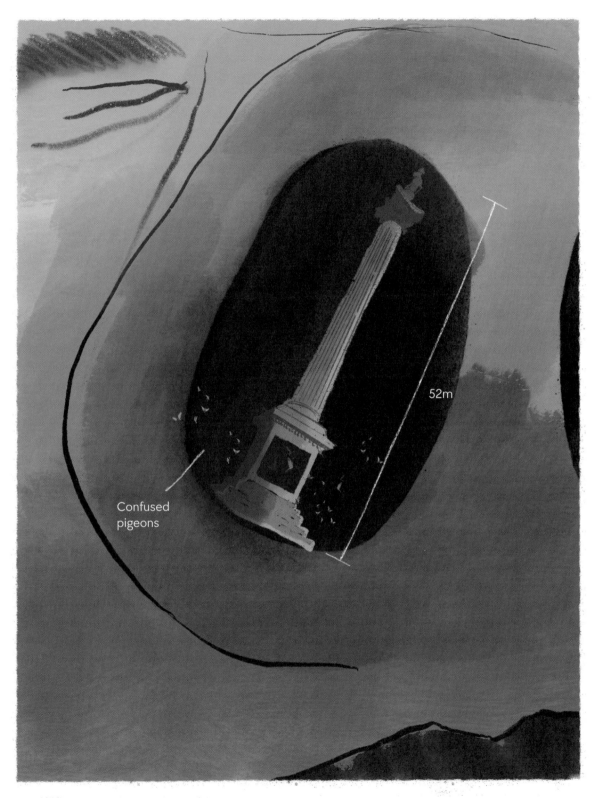

Confused pigeons

52m

And our new mega nostrils are so giant that Nelson's Column could fit inside one. It would tickle though.

With legs this long, we could complete a 40,000-kilometre jog all the way around the planet in three hours flat.

Accidental trail of destruction. Each thumping footstep creates an earthquake registering about a 7 on the Richter scale.

Unless we count astronauts
whizzing around the earth
in space stations, no one's
ever lapped the world this
quickly before.

Then, after our globe trot, we can take a warm salty bath in the middle of the Red Sea to soothe those giant muscles.

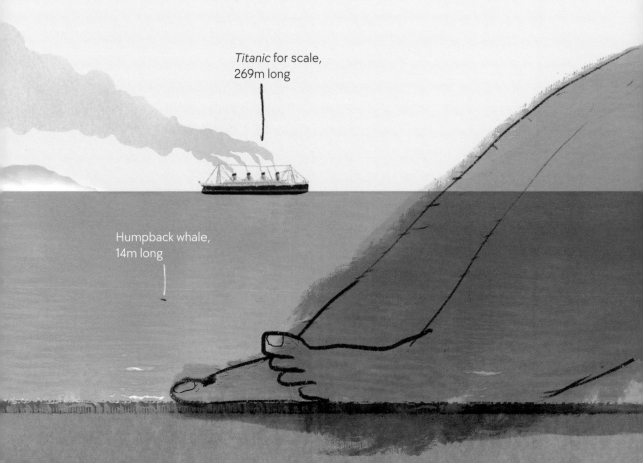

Titanic for scale, 269m long

Humpback whale, 14m long

Average
depth of
Red Sea,
450m

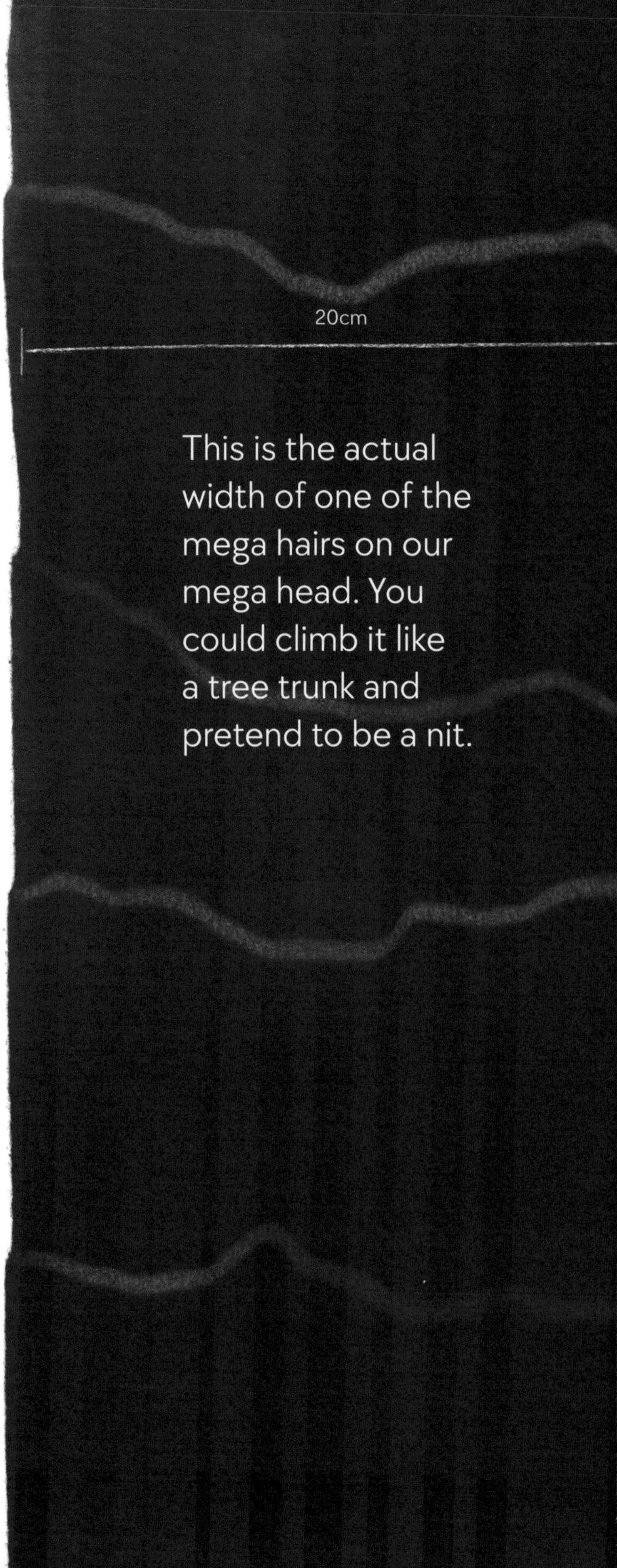

20cm

This is the actual
width of one of the
mega hairs on our
mega head. You
could climb it like
a tree trunk and
pretend to be a nit.

A typical mega hair is between a few
metres and 1.5km long, depending
on when we last had a haircut.

Edge of mega
dandruff particle

Yes, our bodily functions are giant too. Just one mega wee could fill all the canals of Venice. The stream would be taller and more powerful than Angel Falls, which at 979 metres is the highest waterfall in the world.

And our brain? Well, it weighs in at ten million tonnes, measures 330 metres from front to back, and would need the three biggest cargo ships in the world to carry it (and even then, they'd probably sink).

We ought to be very smart indeed.

Our mega brain consumes about the same energy per year as the Netherlands. Pretty efficient, considering it's responsible for all human thought.

Pod of dolphins for scale

Now, while we've got the Smooshing Machine all set up and chugging along, let's throw in some other animals to see how big we are compared to them.

First, we'll coax in all the tigers left in the wild to create the mega tiger.

At 44 metres in length, the mega tiger would be able to leap onto the dome of the Taj Mahal in a single bound and snack on tourists with its rowboat-sized teeth.

The term 'big cat' has never been more fitting.

But the mega tiger is smooshed from the fewer than 4,000 remaining wild tigers. Compared to us, it suddenly doesn't look so huge.

In fact, it can sit comfortably on our mega thumbnail.

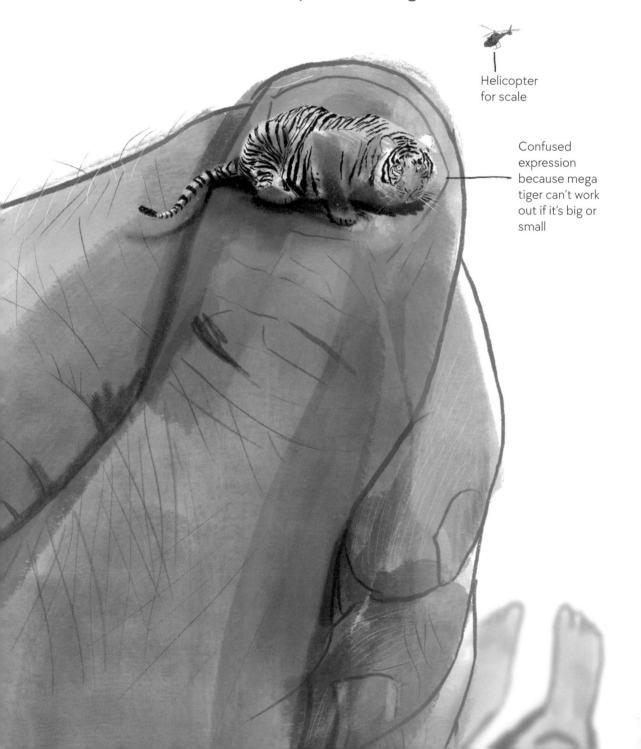

Helicopter for scale

Confused expression because mega tiger can't work out if it's big or small

There are about 25 times as many giraffes in the world as tigers. But a smooshed mega giraffe would still only come up to our ankles.

If all 97,500 giraffes were tempted into the Smooshing Machine with some leafy acacia branches, the resulting mega giraffe would be 230m tall – or 230m short, rather.

Safari truck for scale

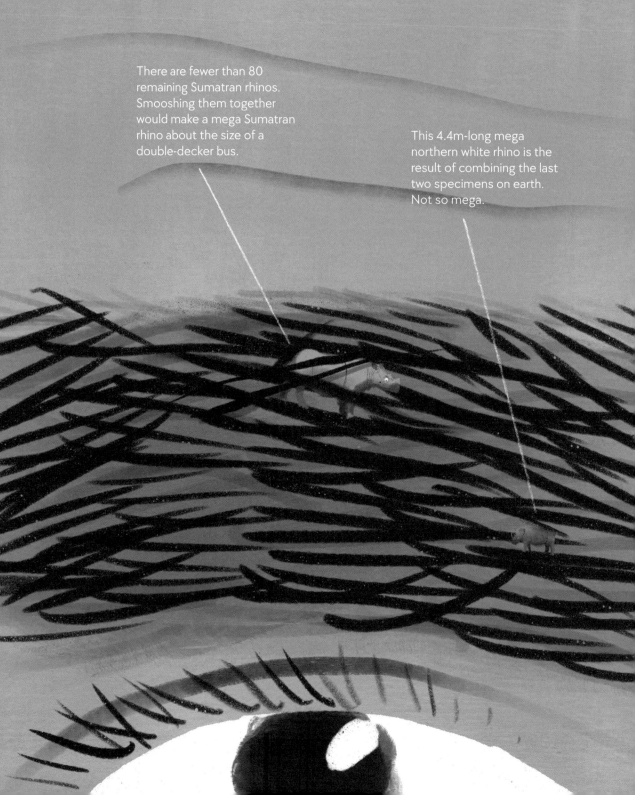

Here's a couple of smooshed rhino species.
You might not see them at first because
they're hiding in our mega eyebrows.

There are fewer than 80
remaining Sumatran rhinos.
Smooshing them together
would make a mega Sumatran
rhino about the size of a
double-decker bus.

This 4.4m-long mega
northern white rhino is the
result of combining the last
two specimens on earth.
Not so mega.

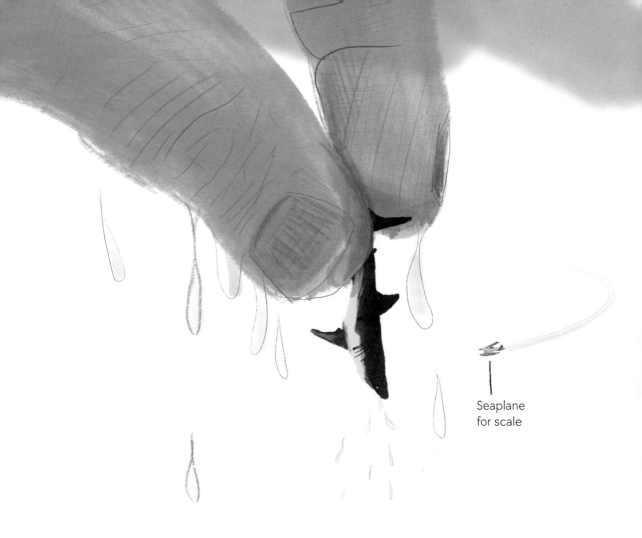

Seaplane
for scale

And here's the 64m-long mega great white shark, made
from all that are left in the sea (estimated at 3,500).
Okay, its jaws could fit around a passenger ferry, but
compared to the mega human it's an anchovy. If
anything, *it* should be making scary movies about *us*.

The mega human isn't the only giant around, though.
The 16-kilometre-tall beast pictured here is the result
of smooshing together all the trillions of microscopic
sea creatures known as copepods.

Sure, the mega copepod is
big – but a lot of its weight
is water. Plus, thousands of
different copepod species
have been combined to make
it. So technically, we're still
probably the #1 biggest
single species of animal.

Well done us!

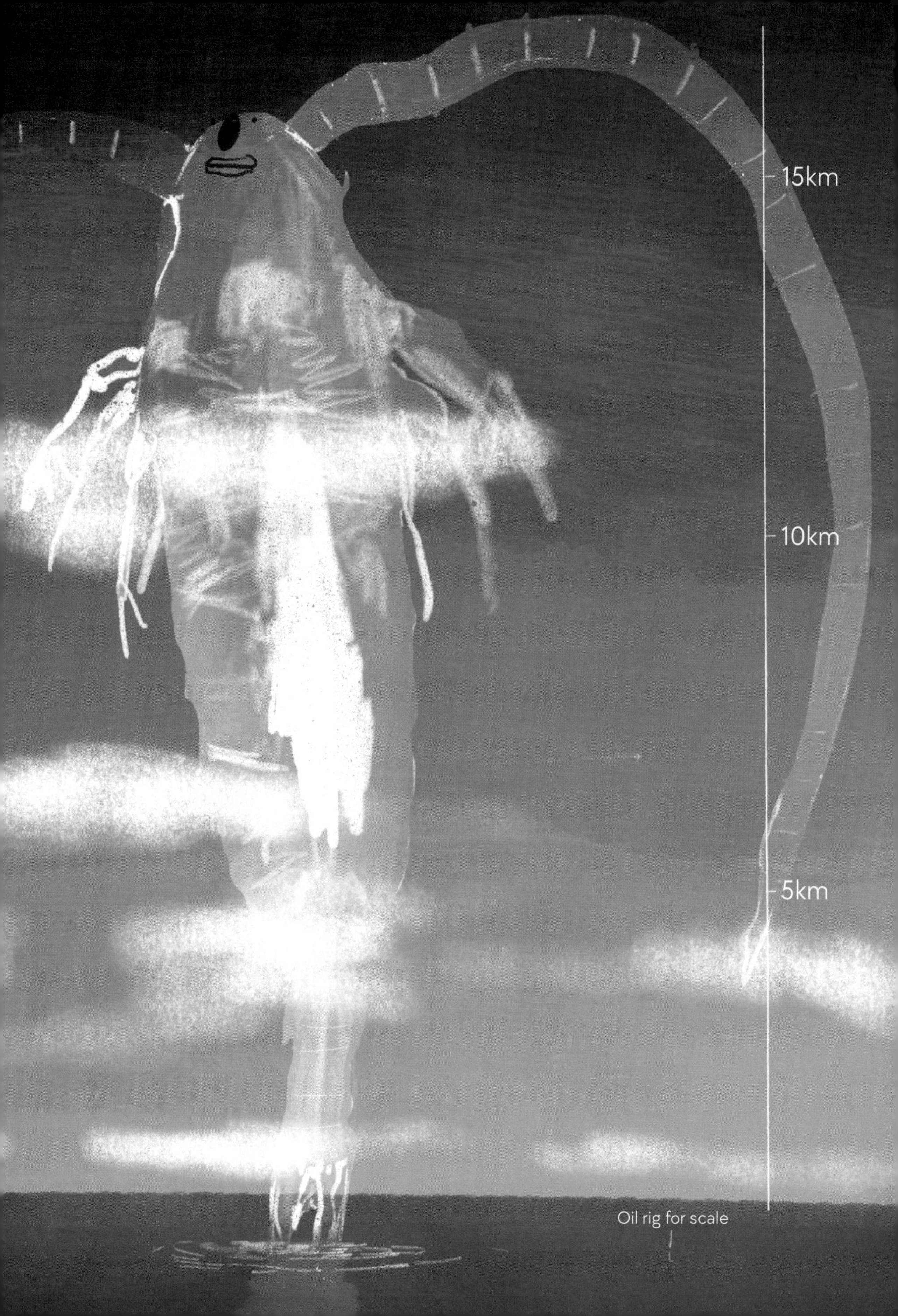

15km

10km

5km

Oil rig for scale

Oh, look! There's a bunch of smooshed mega species having a party in Paris, including a koala doing a King Kong impression. Cute.

Let's go and say bonjour.

From left to right: mega springbok (population 2.25 million), mega giraffe (97,500), mega honeybees in beekeeper-controlled hives (2 trillion), mega emperor penguin (410 million), mega African elephant (415,000), mega giant panda (1,864), mega tiger (3,890), mega monarch butterfly (250 million), mega house sparrow (1.1 billion), mega pygmy three-toed sloth (1,000), mega koala (329,000), mega polar bear (26,500), mega rock dove or common pigeon (260 million) and mega ring-tailed lemur (2,200)

Eiffel Tower, 324m

It seems we aren't too popular with this group.
Only the mega pygmy three-toed sloth is left,
and it's leaving too – just very, very slowly.

Never mind. Those unfriendly species are probably just jealous of how big we are. After all, many of them have been shrinking steadily for decades.

Look how puny the mega African elephant has become over the years!

| 4 km |
| 3 km |
| 2 km |
| 1 km |
| 0 |

1800s

This is what it would have looked like if you had smooshed both species in the 1800s (a billion or so humans and around 26 million elephants). Back then, we were only a bit more jumbo than them.

1900s

As the years passed, we grew apart. More accurately, we grew and they shrank.

Now

Today there are fewer than 500,000 African elephants, whereas our population has doubled, and then doubled again, and then again.

The big ocean dwellers' populations have shrunk even more spectacularly compared to ours. Here's what a sea of smooshed mega marine species would have looked like in 1900:

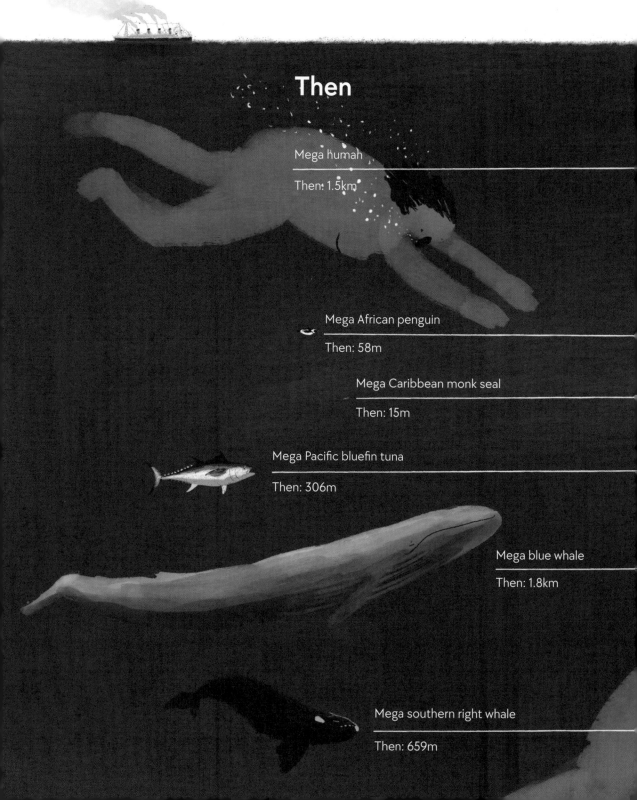

Then

Mega human
Then: 1.5km

Mega African penguin
Then: 58m

Mega Caribbean monk seal
Then: 15m

Mega Pacific bluefin tuna
Then: 306m

Mega blue whale
Then: 1.8km

Mega southern right whale
Then: 659m

And here's what they would look like today.

It's a much lonelier ocean.

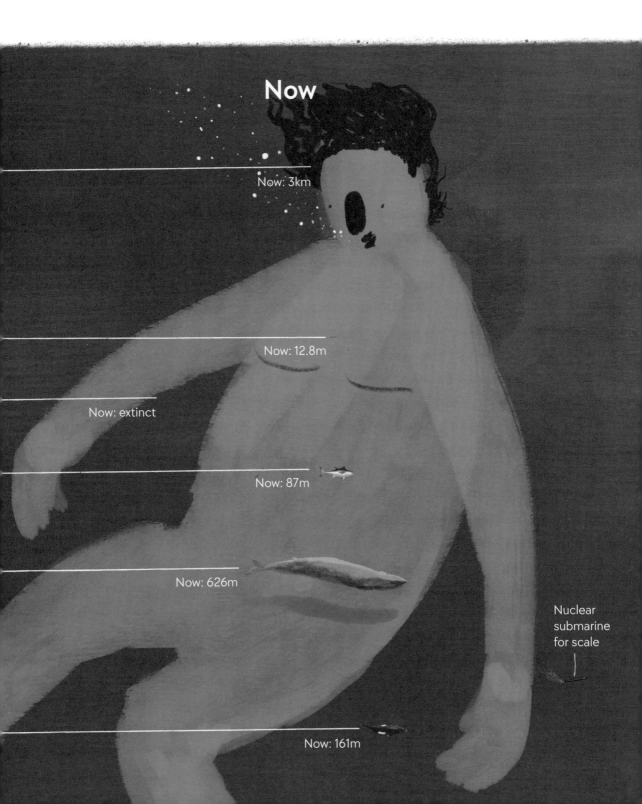

Now

Now: 3km

Now: 12.8m

Now: extinct

Now: 87m

Now: 626m

Nuclear
submarine
for scale

Now: 161m

Maybe we should try hanging out with some friends closer to our own size? Here are a few candidates whose numbers have been rising along with ours.

The first guest at our winners' party is the 1.1km-tall mega chicken. This species is doing so well on our watch (there are 3 chickens for every human) that the mega chicken is 3 times larger than all wild bird populations combined.

The world's cow count has risen to around a billion in the 21st century, making the mega cow another modern heavyweight. Unfortunately for the party, it burps and farts over 4 tonnes of gas every second.

You couldn't say the mega virus is the life of the party. Strictly speaking, it isn't alive at all. Virus particles are tiny, but they're found in every life form, with many living in the sea. The total population of all virus strains is estimated at 10,000,000,000,000,000,000,000,000,000, 000,000, but most are harmless to humans. Even so, pandemics such as Covid-19 mean this 2km-wide party pooper is rarely in our good books.

The mega pig is 855m tall and weighs in at 137 billion tonnes, making it about 3 times heavier than all wild mammals combined. This is another guest who's doing well, thanks to human efforts. Better watch those party nibbles.

Hmm. All our guests may be suited to the modern world, but let's be honest, this party is missing something . . .

The 6.25pm Eurostar service to Brussels, gliding between the mega pig's trotters.

The mega dog!

Our best friend and one true companion animal (even if we did have to breed it especially to like us).

There are around 900 million pet and stray dogs worldwide, from the Afghan hound to the Spitz. Smoosh them together and you get the ultimate mongrel, nearly 500m tall at the shoulders.

We should give the mega dog a name befitting its giant stature, such as Dogzilla. Or how about Noodles?

Oh, Noodles. Not in the seventh arondissement.

We'll just clean that up with a very large poo bag and quickly be on our way.

A single bowel movement by all the world's dogs would look like this and likely cause a strong reaction from residents.

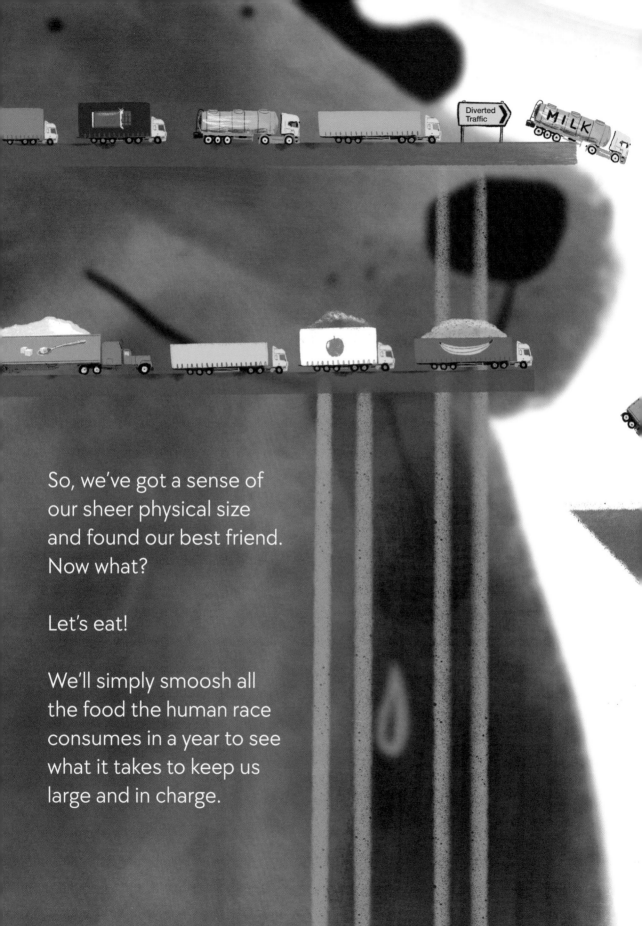

So, we've got a sense of our sheer physical size and found our best friend. Now what?

Let's eat!

We'll simply smoosh all the food the human race consumes in a year to see what it takes to keep us large and in charge.

Inedible material such as wooden pallets, packaging and trucks will be filtered out and removed before smooshing.

This picnic, many times bigger than a city, shows how much of our favourite foods we eat in a year.

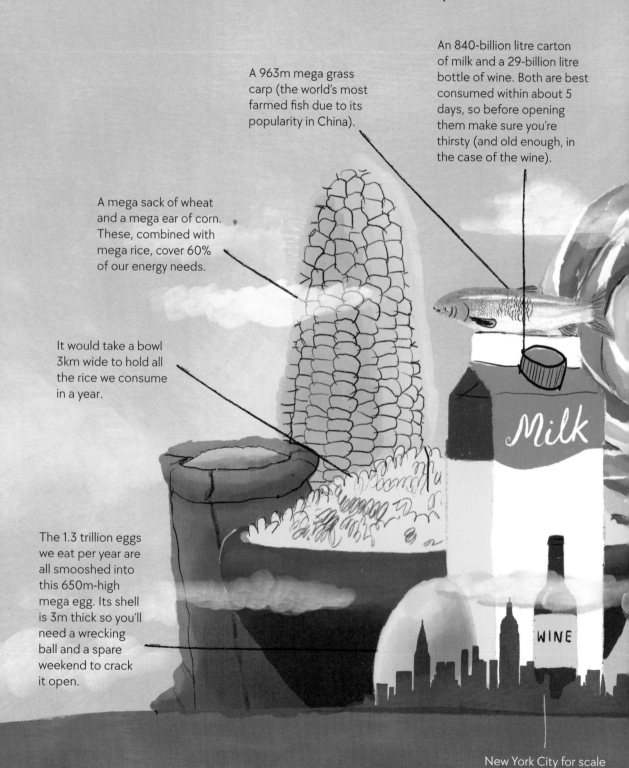

A 963m mega grass carp (the world's most farmed fish due to its popularity in China).

An 840-billion litre carton of milk and a 29-billion litre bottle of wine. Both are best consumed within about 5 days, so before opening them make sure you're thirsty (and old enough, in the case of the wine).

A mega sack of wheat and a mega ear of corn. These, combined with mega rice, cover 60% of our energy needs.

It would take a bowl 3km wide to hold all the rice we consume in a year.

The 1.3 trillion eggs we eat per year are all smooshed into this 650m-high mega egg. Its shell is 3m thick so you'll need a wrecking ball and a spare weekend to crack it open.

Milk

WINE

New York City for scale

This 2.1km-wide lollipop is made with the world's entire yearly sugar cane yield of 1.9 billion tonnes.

The 'wartime delicacy' Spam is still going strong today, with an equivalent of a 60m can of the stuff being produced every year.

The succulent 160-million-tonne mega tomato. We process about a quarter of this into tomato sauce, tomato paste and tomato juice.

Work up an appetite with a 3km jog around the mega roast chicken. It would just about fit in Central Park.

A 1.2km-tall mega bottle of palm oil. This stuff gets everywhere. You can find it, often listed under another name, on the ingredients list for anything from packaged bread, peanut butter and pizza to chocolate, ice cream and sweets.

The 450m mega avocado tastes delicious on an acre of toast.

Let's take a closer look at one particular recipe, perhaps humanity's greatest culinary creation.

The mega burger

Serves: All humanity
(or more accurately the 6 billion who eat meat)

Time to make: 1 year

1. Find a patch of empty land about the size of Europe. You may have to clear a few forests first but it's worth the extra preparation time.

2. Sow liberally (you'll need several trillion seeds).

3. Fertilise and sprinkle with water every day for two to four months.

4 quadrillion litres of water

Soup lake

Mammoth Tacos

Chicago-sized pizza

Easy recipes for your entire species

4. Collect your nice pile of food . . .

5. . . . feed it to your mega livestock animals . . .

6. . . . and feed them into a grinder . . .

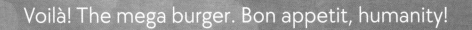

Voilà! The mega burger. Bon appetit, humanity!

Hot-air
balloon
for scale

Mega patty made
from all the meat
humans produce in
a year, 1.8km across

Serving suggestion: place mega burger
on top of Table Mountain in South Africa
(2.5km across)

After putting so much work into it, you can be sure we'll savour every last bi–

Oh.

Sure, we can be a bit wasteful – but not to worry, we're also doing lots of things to be a better giant, like eating alternatives to meat. That's got to be a step in the right direction, hasn't it?

Mega halo, 500m wide

I ♥ EARTH

Eden Project for scale (home to the world's largest indoor rainforest)

The mega electric car, 765m long, made by smooshing all the electric cars currently on the road.

Mega veggie sausage roll the size of a giant skyscraper, made from all the pea protein produced in a year: 430m long and growing fast.

A sustainable way to get around: the mega bike, smooshed from an estimated 2 billion bicycles in use today.

565m-high mega compactor lorry, holding all of the plastic the world recycles in a year in crushed form.

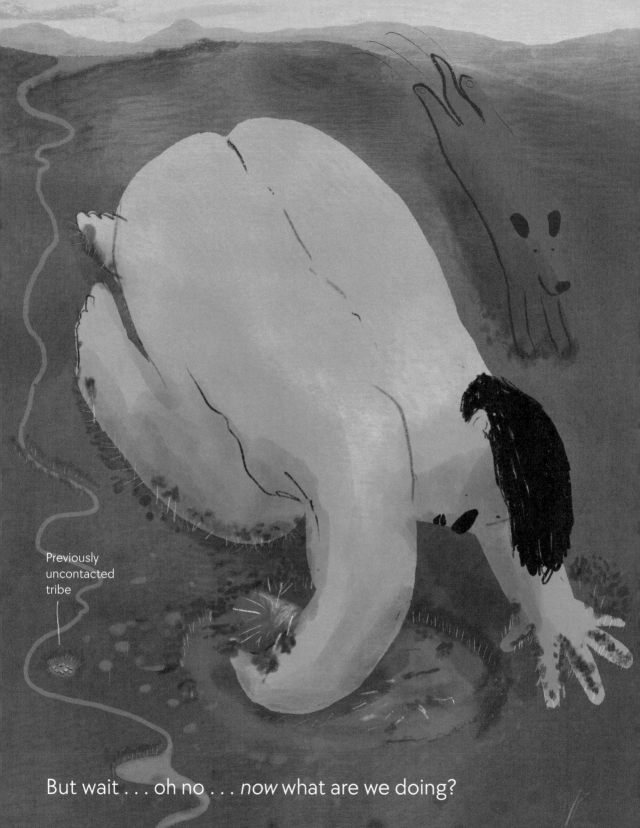

Previously
uncontacted
tribe

But wait . . . oh no . . . *now* what are we doing?

It looks like we're indulging in one of our favourite activities:
digging up a place of great natural beauty.

For us, digging is more than a hobby.

It's a passion.

Maybe even an addiction.

But what are we digging for? Only one of our all-time most treasured substances: gold.

All the gold ever mined would create a pile around 24m high. Think of all the wars caused by this sparkly little hill.

Fort Knox for scale (where the US keeps its gold reserves)

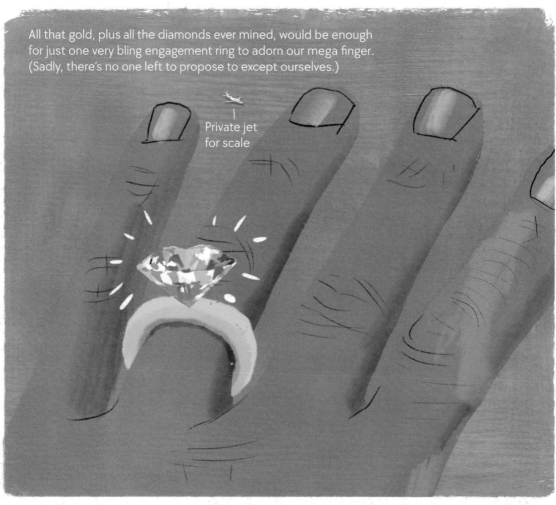

All that gold, plus all the diamonds ever mined, would be enough for just one very bling engagement ring to adorn our mega finger. (Sadly, there's no one left to propose to except ourselves.)

Private jet for scale

We're digging for rare minerals like dysprosium, yttrium and tantalum, which we use to make the inner workings of our beloved electronic devices.

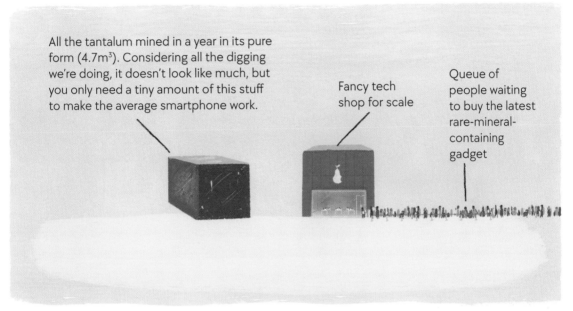

All the tantalum mined in a year in its pure form (4.7m³). Considering all the digging we're doing, it doesn't look like much, but you only need a tiny amount of this stuff to make the average smartphone work.

Fancy tech shop for scale

Queue of people waiting to buy the latest rare-mineral-containing gadget

67m-tall mega western lowland gorilla, not very happy about the hole where its nest used to be.

Open-pit mines

The magnificent mega smartphone is 220m tall with a display as big as a hundred cinema screens. It's about the only thing on the planet capable of distracting us from digging.

We're also digging for massive quantities of sand and gravel.

Why? So we can make enough cement, concrete and glass to put up millions of new buildings every year.

Mount Everest
for scale

All the sand and gravel
extracted from the
earth in one year

Behold the mega human's latest construction project: the mega tower. This is what it would look like if all the new floorspace the human race creates globally in twelve months, estimated at six billion m^2, were smooshed into a single skyscraper 10,000 storeys high.

The cafe on the top floor, 40km in the sky, is a 40-minute journey from ground level by high-speed express elevator. You'd need a space suit to visit or your blood would start to boil, but the views are out of this world.

The world's tallest and highest capacity buildings for scale (easy to ignore when situated next door to the mega tower)

After all that, we still have enough construction materials spare each year to pave over an area the size of Croatia (56,000km^2). Plenty of room to land the mega plane and park a mega automobile made of all the petrol, diesel and electric cars in the world combined.

Heathrow Airport Terminal 5 for scale

And, last but not least, we're digging for fossil fuels: coal, gas and oil.

Every year, we burn through a 2.8km-high barrel full of oil, a 3km-high coal mountain and 4,000km³ of natural gas.

Oil truck for scale

We're burning so much, in fact, that the whole planet is beginning to suffer from breathing difficulties.

It's not just smog and smoke, either. Fossil fuels also give off 35 billion tonnes of invisible, odourless CO_2 per year, making them the biggest cause of climate change.

From this satellite view, you can see we've dug a pit of over 60 cubic kilometres. That's the volume of resources humans dig out of the earth's surface every year.

Or picture it this way: every single second, we scoop an entire swimming pool of stone, sand, clay, minerals, fossil fuels, metals and organic matter out of our increasingly pockmarked planet. We just can't seem to stop.

And digging isn't our only hobby.
We also like to chop down trees.
Around 15 billion of them a year,
in fact.

If you smooshed all the trees
we cut down in 12 months,
we'd have felled a mega tree
about 35km in height and
2.5km around the trunk at
the base. If you cut it down in
England it could make a bridge
across the Channel to France.

As a tree lover,
Noodles wants
no part in this.

Burj Khalifa for scale
(world's tallest
building, 830m)

All this chopping gives us a lot of timber and wood pulp. Enough to make 330 billion toilet rolls, a 1.5km-high bonfire, or this hugely handy 8km-tall mega flatpack bookcase.

(Which, now we've put it up, we realise we didn't really need and doesn't match our curtains.)

This should really be fixed to a wall to prevent toppling.

HÜM

We've gained a practical storage solution for our mega ornaments. Unfortunately, rather a lot of forest-dwelling mega species have lost their homes, such as (shown here fleeing) the mega Bornean orangutan (59m tall), mega southern cassowary (37m), and mega great green macaw (11m).

In case the scale of the trouble we're causing isn't clear by now, let's not forget the plastic we dump in the sea.

Weight equivalent of 100 plastic bottles per human, per year

And the clothes we chuck away after a couple of wears.

These size XXXXXXL polyester leggings went from catwalk to stores in two weeks, but will take 200 years to decompose.

FASHION VICTIM

And the wildlife we illegally trade.

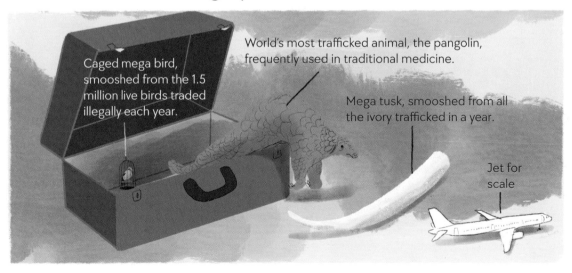

Caged mega bird, smooshed from the 1.5 million live birds traded illegally each year.

World's most trafficked animal, the pangolin, frequently used in traditional medicine.

Mega tusk, smooshed from all the ivory trafficked in a year.

Jet for scale

Hmm. Maybe all this digging, burning, building, dumping, wasting and poaching has something to do with why so many mega species have been shrinking and disappearing lately?

From left to right: mega emperor penguin (population 410 million), mega western lowland gorilla (100,000), mega giraffe (97,500), mega African elephant (415,000), mega duck-billed platypus (165,000). Also depicted but difficult to see are the mega vaquita porpoise (14) and the mega Hainan black crested gibbon (28). When you're our size, species this small are easy to overlook.

The puff symbols represent recent extinctions such as the splendid poison frog, Jalpa false brook salamander and the smooth handfish.

The truth is, we're a bit of a mess.

And to cap it all, it looks like we're coming down with a nasty virus.

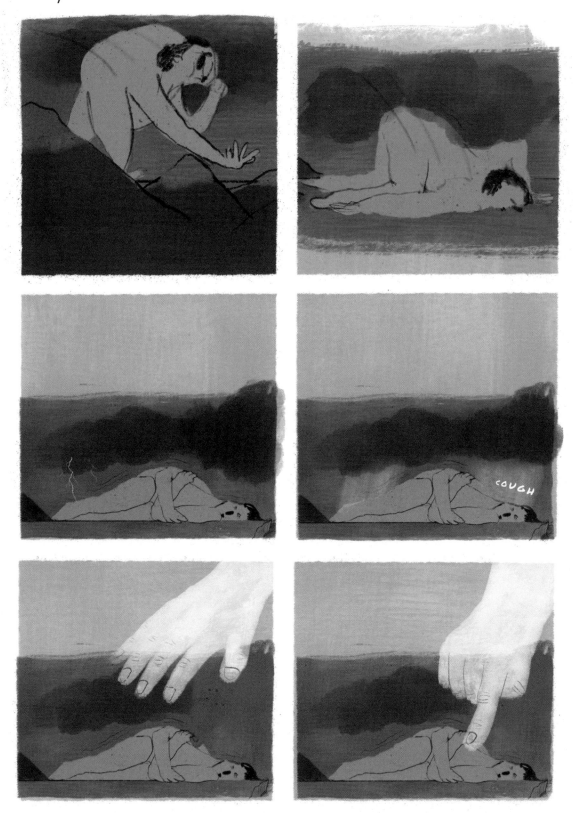

Whoa. Are we having a fever dream?

Or could it be we're receiving a visit from the mega ghost, made up of all 99 billion humans who lived before us?

So, folks, what the heck is going on? I leave you alone for a few generations and you've trashed the place. In my day we took what we needed and lived in harmony with other species. Okay, some scientists think we hunted various large mammals to extinction in the Stone Age, but nothing's been proven. Besides, we needed the mammoth meat – we didn't have your fancy technology, like farming. Anyway, this isn't about me. There's someone I'd like you to meet . . .

Gulp.

Now, who is this strange 70-kilometre-tall beast?!

Put every living thing into the Smooshing Machine – every tree, every bird, every blade of grass, every germ – and this is who comes out. Its name is ALOE: All Life on Earth.

ALOE is ten thousand times bigger than you, a lot older, and wiser too (in a plant-y sort of way). In fact, you're a part of ALOE: you could be a pimple on its hindquarters.

Yet somewhere along the line, you decided you were big and clever enough to go it alone, with no thought for how your actions would affect your giant friend here. Well, guess what, kiddo. If you can't figure out how to live in harmony with ALOE, you've got some dark and hungry days ahead of you.

Now, there's one more thing I want to show you . . .

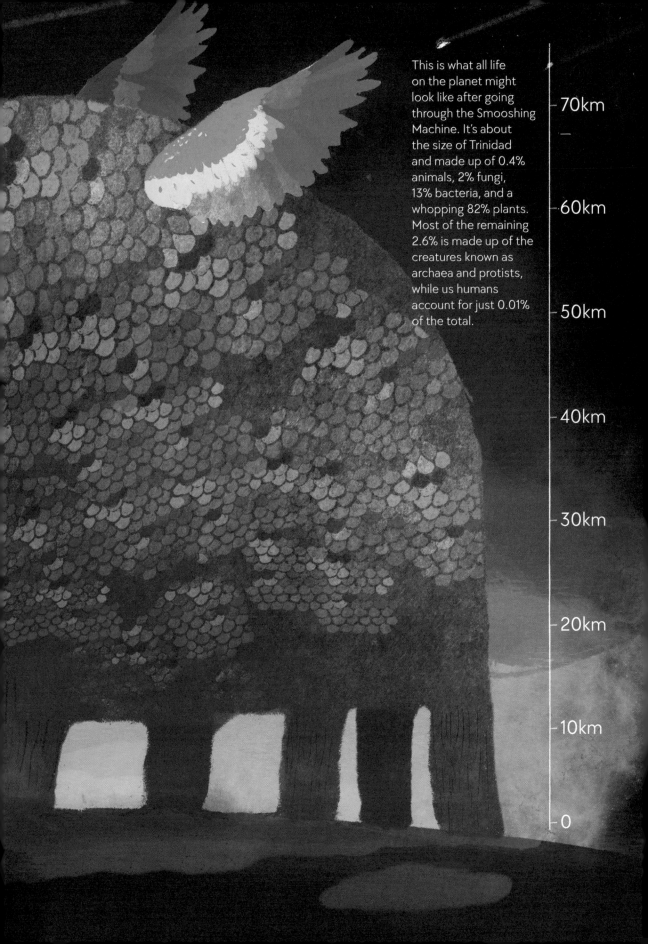

This is what all life on the planet might look like after going through the Smooshing Machine. It's about the size of Trinidad and made up of 0.4% animals, 2% fungi, 13% bacteria, and a whopping 82% plants. Most of the remaining 2.6% is made up of the creatures known as archaea and protists, while us humans account for just 0.01% of the total.

70km

60km

50km

40km

30km

20km

10km

0

Huh?

Why is the mega ghost showing us
this immense heap of junk?!

I present to you:
all your stuff. That's
right, everything on
earth that's been
manufactured by
humans, all rolled up
into a ball. And look
how much of it there is!
Scientists reckon that
the human-made world
is now more massive
than the living one. In
other words, despite
the fact that you're only
a teensy little part of
ALOE, your things weigh
even more than it does.
And every day, ALOE
slowly shrinks so that
you can keep making
your precious hunk of
junk bigger. Is that really
how you want to live
your life? Well, is it?!

On average, the mega human produces
materials equal to our entire body weight
every week. This stuff ranges from concrete
and metal to plastic and tarmac, from palaces
and bus stations to statues and sofas.

Here's a strange thought: although this is a scene of
epic proportions, if everything living and everything
human-made were brought together like this, they'd
easily fit on an island the size of Madagascar, leaving
the rest of earth as a rocky, lifeless landscape.

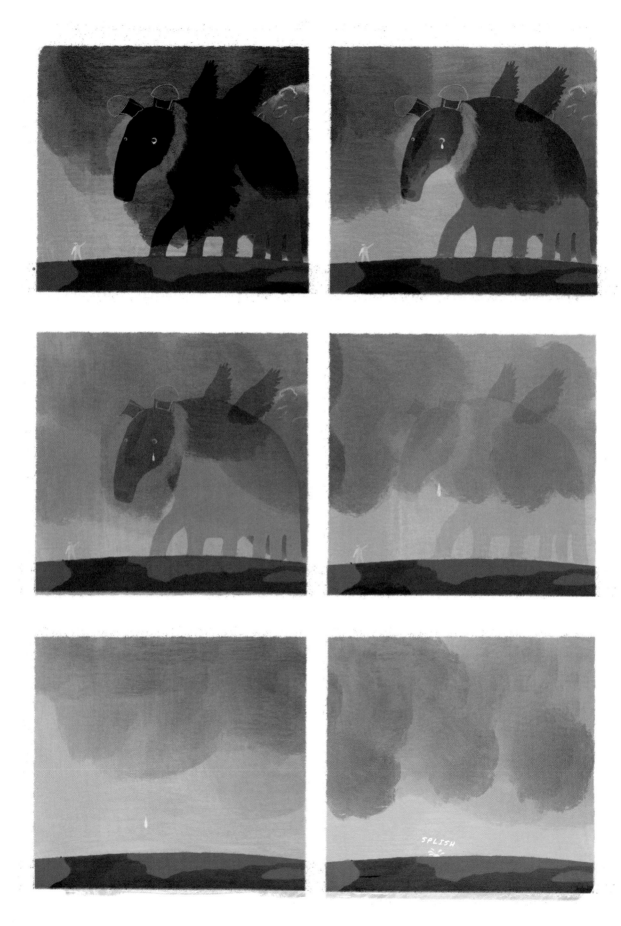

As dreams go, that was pretty weird.

Maybe the mega ghost was right. Even giants can get too big for their boots.

No wonder Noodles ran away.

But there's no use being gloomy. It's not our fault we're not perfect.

At least our fever has passed.

Now, what were we doing?
Ah yes, digging.

Let's go and start a new pit –
that usually distracts us.

Who's this we nearly trod on?

Hop up, small green bird.

There's a forested spot over here where you'll be safer.

The mega kakapo, raising a grateful claw. Thanks to recent conservation efforts, this flightless parrot's numbers have slowly risen back to triple figures.

See you later, little one.

Wait a second. That actually felt kind of good.

It looks like we're having one of our mega ideas (like writing down words – that was a classic).

What if we treated the entire planet with the care and respect we just showed that rare parrot?

We'd need to stop acting on our more selfish impulses (of which there are billions zinging through our mega mind at any one time).

And we'd need to start following through on our good intentions. We've got a tendency to ignore those.

But if our entire massive brain could get behind our new goal, and our whole galumphing body could work on it as one . . . who knows what we might achieve?

We could plant loads of new trees . . .

A trillion of these would lock away 10 years of carbon emissions.

. . . clean the plastic from the oceans . . .

This would make marine life very happy.

. . . and find a better way to create power.

More wind turbines like these could reduce our need for fossil fuels.

We could give back to the places we've taken from.

* Strassburg, B.B.N., Iribarrem, A., Beyer, H.L. et al. Global priority areas for ecosystem restoration. *Nature* 586, 724–9 (2020)

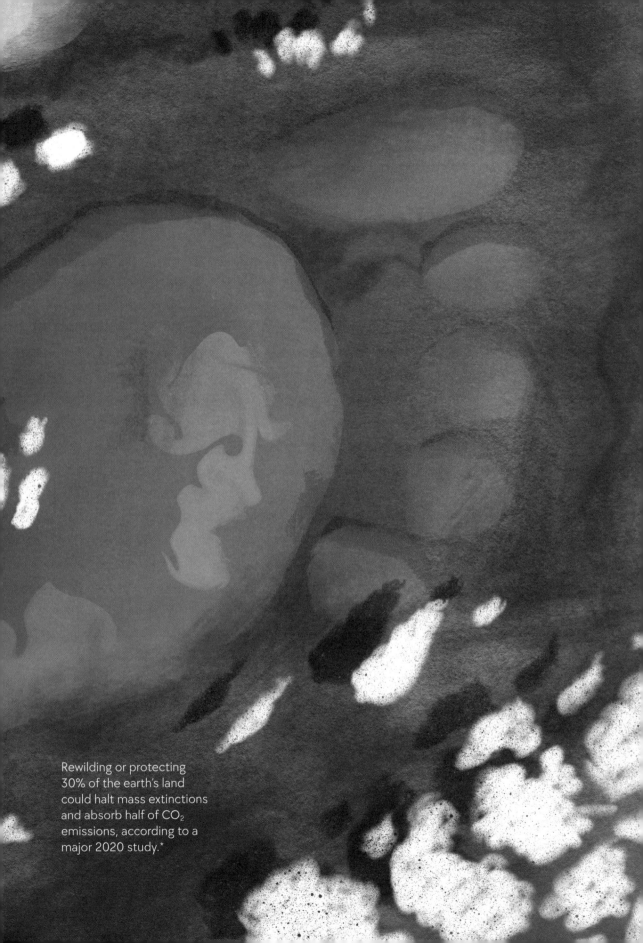

Rewilding or protecting 30% of the earth's land could halt mass extinctions and absorb half of CO_2 emissions, according to a major 2020 study.*

Then we really would be able to call ourselves an amazing species.

We might even find peace with our fellow mega creatures.

Lakeside
eco centre

From left to right: mega giraffe (population 97,500), mega Grandidier's baobab tree (1 million), mega Canada goose (5.1 million), mega elk (2 million), mega red-billed quelea (1.5 billion), mega king eider duck (population 870,000), mega Indian peafowl (100,000), mega freshwater crocodile (100,000), mega plains zebra (200,000), mega Bornean orangutan (104,700), mega African elephant (415,000)

Hey, look! Noodles has bounded back to snap us out of our daydream. Just as well – we've got work to do.

We can count on humankind's best friend to forgive us. But there are still 8.7 million mega species left to win over. (That's the estimated total number of animal, plant, algae and fungi species on the planet, all of whom are affected by our activities.)

This is going to be a big challenge.

Maybe even impossibly big.

But if we can make the mega burger and build the mega building and dig the mega pit, maybe we can take on the even bigger job of fixing the mega mess we've made.

And even if we can't, don't we owe it to the planet to try?

It's time we de-smooshed ourselves. After all, we've got no time to lose, and billions of hands must be better than two – no matter how giant.

We'll do some stretches . . .

. . . switch the Smooshing Machine to reverse . . .

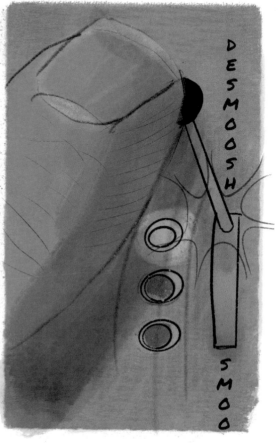

DESMOOSH

SMOO

. . . give ourselves the biggest high five in history, audible for hundreds of miles . . .

. . . climb into the de-smooshing funnel . . .

Professor McCrackers, leading humanity back out of her amazing machine.

Come on, everyone! No time for the gift shop: we've got a job to do.

. . . and out we pour! (You may feel a warm tingle as you separate from the rest of humankind.)

And here we are again. Every single one of us.

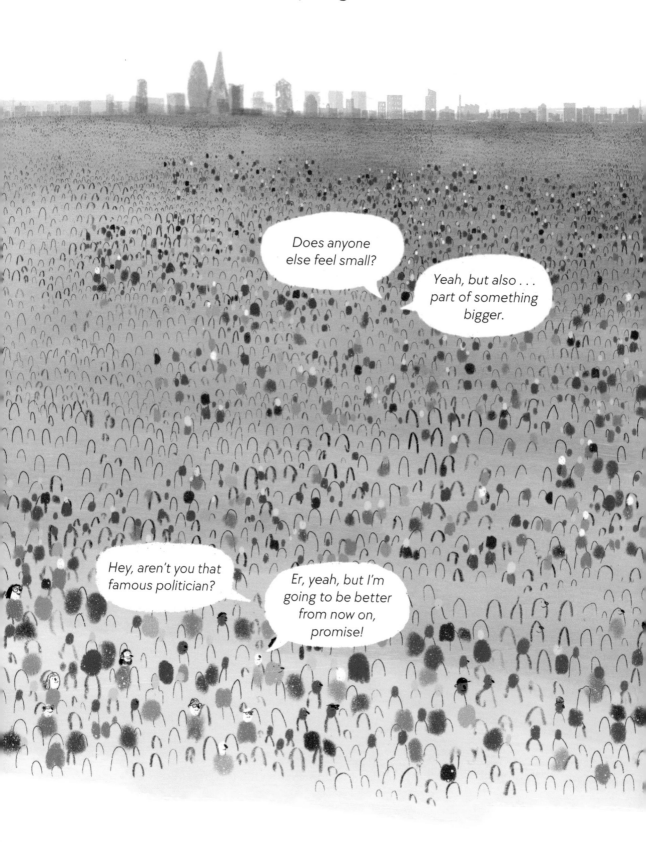

Un-de-smooshed animals pictured in background: mega emperor penguin (population 410 million) and mega domestic cat (600 million).

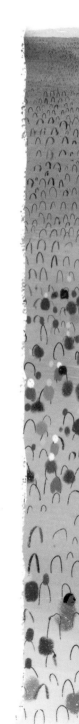

For being part of this experiment we would like to thank the entire human race, but most especially Claire and Grace for their amazing ideas and patience; Otto, who made it really difficult for Tom to finish this book but in a fun way; and our mum and dad for all the plants, socks and moral support.

Thanks also to Hannah, Jamie, Jenny, Leila, Vicki, Aa'Ishah, Alice, Valeri, Kate, Nick, Lois, Alison and all at Canongate; Gordon and Niall at Curtis Brown; and everyone who helped with early drafts.

Acknowledgements are due to all the scientists and organisations on whose research we have relied, especially the International Union for Conservation of Nature for their wildlife population estimates, and the Food and Agriculture Organization of the United Nations for their incredible database of food production statistics.

If you're interested in more of the facts, figures and theory behind Professor McCrackers' Smooshing Machine, or things you can do to help us become a better giant, please visit The Biggest Footprint website:

thebiggestfootprint.com

First published in Great Britain in 2021 by Canongate Books Ltd, 14 High Street, Edinburgh EH1 1TE

canongate.co.uk

1

British Library Cataloguing-in-Publication Data
A catalogue record for this book is available on request from the British Library

ISBN 978 1 83885 349 5

Typesetting by Nick Venables

Printed and bound in China by 1010 Printing Ltd